IMAGES
of America

FORT MONROE

This image is part of a sequence of pictures captured by photographer J. A. Wilson on March 10, 1913, under the supervision of Capt. F. J. Behr, director of Enlisted Specialists at the Coast Artillery School. It offers a rare glimpse of a 12-inch mortar being test fired inside either Battery Anderson or Battery Ruggles at Fort Monroe. Wilson used an exposure of 1/5000 of a second to film the launching of a 900-miles-per-hour projectile, which is visible above the smoke. (Courtesy of the Casemate Museum.)

ON THE COVER: A young artilleryman poses on the carriage of one of the many 10-inch Rodman guns inside Fort Monroe's Water Battery, c. 1890. The Water Battery provided additional firepower to the fort's existing arsenal, further securing the Hampton Roads waterway. It was demolished in 1907, with only the powder magazine now barely standing. (Courtesy of the Casemate Museum.)

IMAGES
of America

FORT MONROE

Paul S. Morando and David J. Johnson

ARCADIA
PUBLISHING

Copyright © 2008 by Paul S. Morando and David J. Johnson
ISBN 978-0-7385-6734-1

Published by Arcadia Publishing
Charleston SC, Chicago IL, Portsmouth NH, San Francisco CA

Printed in the United States of America

Library of Congress Catalog Card Number: 2008927940

For all general information contact Arcadia Publishing at:
Telephone 843-853-2070
Fax 843-853-0044
E-mail sales@arcadiapublishing.com
For customer service and orders:
Toll-Free 1-888-313-2665

Visit us on the Internet at www.arcadiapublishing.com

This 1934 view of the entire fort looks quite different from more recent images. The seawall
has not yet been constructed. The Hotel Chamberlin still has its twin domes, and there is no
marina. The great landfill projects along Mill Creek and the Chesapeake Bay are still in the
future. The present Sherwood Park can be seen as just a big vacant lot following the demolition
of the Sherwood Inn in 1932. (Courtesy of the Casemate Museum.)

CONTENTS

Acknowledgments		6
Introduction		7
1.	A New Beginning: 1865–1890	9
2.	Modernizing Fort Monroe: 1891–1916	21
3.	Fort Monroe in the Great War: 1917–1919	45
4.	Challenges: 1920–1940	59
5.	Training for War: 1941–1945	79
6.	An Era Ends and New Missions Begin: 1946–1972	99
7.	The Road Ahead: 1973–Present	113

ACKNOWLEDGMENTS

The vast majority of images published in this book came from the Casemate Museum archives. We also received additional material from several Fort Monroe organizations. We would particularly like to thank Patrick Buffett from the Fort Monroe Public Affairs Office, Eva Granville and Kathleen Miller from U.S. Army Community Services, Paul Presenza from the Public Works Environmental Office, and 1st Lt. Sharon Toulouse from the Training and Doctrine Command (TRADOC) Band.

Assistance was also provided by two local institutions: the Hampton University Library and the Mariners' Museum. We are especially grateful to Michael Cobb and Bethany Austin of the Hampton History Museum for their cooperation in this project. In addition, Dr. Charles Cureton from the TRADOC History Office, Dennis Mroczkowski from the Center of Military History, and Richard Cox from the Harbor Defense Museum were very helpful in the preparation of this book. The author would especially like to thank his wife, Holly Morando, for her constant support.

A gun crew at Battery Irwin poses with a 3-inch, armored, rapid-fire gun around 1915. Near the upper left corner of the image is the Hotel Chamberlin. Directly behind the crewmembers are the lighthouse keeper's cottage, a fog bell, and the Old Point Comfort lighthouse. Battery Irwin's armament was removed after World War I. (Courtesy of Hampton History Museum.)

INTRODUCTION

At the entrance of Hampton Roads, where the Atlantic Ocean and the James River converge at the mouth of the Chesapeake Bay, stands an American castle. Fort Monroe, with its brick arches and solid granite walls, looms over the sea as a powerful symbol of America's national defense system.

The ramparts and casemates are no longer filled with large seacoast guns. What remains are the rusted gun rails on which the wooden carriages traversed—remnants of Fort Monroe's military past. The only constant is the water in the moat that slowly moves along the outer walls of the fort. It is a sustaining presence, always there like Fort Monroe's history itself, ebbing and flowing with the tide.

Named after the fifth president of the United States, James Monroe, the fort's size speaks for itself. The walls stretch 1.3 miles around, enclosing 63 acres of land to become known as the "Gibraltar of the Chesapeake."

During the construction of Fort Monroe (1819–1834) some critics denounced its size as being too big and a waste of government funds (overall cost was more than $1.8 million) while others saw it as a monumental achievement in military engineering. Nevertheless, Fort Monroe had an integral part in the history of the United States and was a witness to and participant in many significant events.

This book does not set out to cover the entire story of Fort Monroe, which is more appropriate for a formal publication. A chapter could be dedicated to the founding of Point Comfort (the small peninsula that Fort Monroe sits on) by English colonists in 1607. Capt. John Smith called this area an "Isle fit for a Castle" in 1608 after establishing the colony of Jamestown. Another chapter easily could highlight the fortifications that were built here prior to Fort Monroe to include Fort Algernourne (1609–1612), Point Comfort Fort (1632–1667), and Fort George (1727–1749).

More importantly, another chapter could uncover why the army built Fort Monroe. The need for a nationalized permanent system of fortifications came right after the War of 1812. After escaping defeat at the hands of the British, U.S. military leaders, and politicians realized that their defenses were inadequate to repel a formidable attack. A prime example of this vulnerability came in August 1814. After burning the city of Hampton, Virginia, in 1813, the British easily sailed up the Chesapeake Bay and burned Washington, D.C. As a counterpoint, the Battle of Baltimore (September 12–15, 1814) emphasized the importance of having strong, well-built fortifications at key locations. Fort McHenry proved useful in keeping the British at bay, thus preventing them from entering the Baltimore harbor and capturing the city. These events, along with the rise of Napoleon in Europe, compelled the young United States to begin a calculated strategy of defending its shores, coastal areas, ports, and cities.

Another chapter could also describe Fort Monroe's involvement in Nat Turner's Rebellion (1831), the Indian Wars (1832–1836), and the Mexican War (1846–1848). Focus could also be placed on the many famous individuals who were either stationed here or passed through Fort Monroe, including Edgar Allan Poe, Chief Black Hawk, Robert E. Lee, Benjamin Butler, Abraham Lincoln, and Jefferson Davis. The variety of historical buildings on the installation could be highlighted, featuring architecture in the art deco, Romanesque, Beaux-Arts, Colonial Revival, Empire, Federal, and Gothic Revival styles. Moreover, Fort Monroe's most important period, the Civil War, with events such as the contraband decision, the Battle of Big Bethel, and the Peninsula Campaign has already been covered extensively in another Arcadia publication, *Fort Monroe: The Key to the South.*

The purpose of this book is to complete the story by capturing the history of Fort Monroe from the end of the Civil War (1865) to the Department of Defense's decision to place Fort Monroe on the Base Realignment and Closure (BRAC) list in 2005. This book reveals through photographs how Fort Monroe adapted and overcame many challenges. From changing military technology and new missions, to hurricanes and budget setbacks, Fort Monroe and the U.S. Army have always managed to continue on.

In 1865, with the rest of the nation still reeling from the aftermath of the Civil War, Fort Monroe was trying to define its role as an army installation by adapting new missions and abandoning old ones. The Artillery School of Practice, established by Brig. Gen. Abraham Eustis in 1824, was put on hold during the war. It was revived as the Artillery School of the United States Army and trained soldiers on artillery tactics using field and seacoast cannons, as well as teaching basic military courses. Fort Monroe also became a destination for many tourists with the construction of the second Hygeia Hotel in 1868. During this time, a local chapter of the "Freedmen's Bureau" was created on Fort Monroe to help with Reconstruction that gave aid to thousands of former slaves.

From 1891 to 1916, Fort Monroe went through a modernization of its coastal defenses, which had a profound effect on its mission. The smoothbore cannons inside the casemates and on the ramparts were no longer effective. Even the powerful 15-inch Rodman guns and 100-pounder Parrott guns were outclassed by modern guns available at the turn of the 20th century. New emphasis was now placed on the development of large disappearing guns housed in concrete batteries that were capable of firing 1,070-pound projectiles eight miles. These new weapons replaced the need for having large stone forts as part of America's national defense system. In 1907, the Coast Artillery School was established at Fort Monroe and went on to train thousands of soldiers for the next 40 years. The urgency of World War I transformed Fort Monroe into a Coast Artillery Training Center to prepare officers and enlisted men for service overseas.

The two decades before World War II proved to be a difficult time for Fort Monroe. The onset of the Great Depression reduced military spending, and the installation witnessed the burning of the Hotel Chamberlin in 1920 and suffered through a major hurricane in 1933. However, Fort Monroe prevailed and began to rebuild in 1934, and continued its coast artillery training mission.

Another era in military technology entered Fort Monroe during World War II. The advent of air and sea power brought about the development of new types of weapons, including submarine mines and the use of anti-aircraft artillery. By this time, the large steel disappearing guns, like the smoothbore cannons of the Civil War, were beginning to be phased out. In 1942, a major scrap drive added to the reduction of these weapons.

The years after World War II also had a tremendous impact on Fort Monroe. Air power made the Coast Artillery Corps obsolete, and the U.S. War Department disbanded it on January 1, 1950. With it went a long tradition of military training that defined and sustained Fort Monroe for decades.

In 1955, Fort Monroe became the home of the headquarters for the Continental Army Command (CONARC). During this time, effort was also put into preserving the history of Fort Monroe with the establishment of the Casemate Museum in 1951 and Fort Monroe's designation as a National Historic Landmark on December 19, 1960.

On July 1, 1973, Fort Monroe became the headquarters for the Training and Doctrine Command (TRADOC) under the command of Gen. William E. DePuy. This command oversees army training throughout the United States.

Fort Monroe is a survivor. The images in this book illustrate the dynamics of how a historic military installation evolved over time. Fort Monroe has endured technological changes, hurricanes, fires, budget restrictions, and new mission requirements to continue on as a vital part of the army's role in defending the United States.

The closure of Fort Monroe in 2011, ending 192 years of service for the U. S. Army at Old Point Comfort, will once again present a new set of challenges. Over the years, Fort Monroe's resiliency and toughness led to its success; it defined its character. Now it seems fated for a new course. The impenetrable granite walls of the fort have always been a protector, first as a physical structure—its presence alone mitigated any real attacks from enemy naval ships—and now as a symbol of strength and fortitude in a new era of crisis.

It can be argued that more natural disasters, financial issues, and unknown problems could continue to threaten the fort's existence. The future of Fort Monroe is uncertain, but like the water in the moat, its history will forever encompass the fort.

One

A NEW BEGINNING

1865–1890

The conclusion of the Civil War brought an end to major military activity in the United States. In fact, the entire U.S. Army fell into a period of stagnation. However, amidst this transition to peacetime, on November 13, 1867, Fort Monroe was able to re-establish the Artillery School of Practice (1824), renamed the Artillery School of the United States Army. Col. William F. Barry, a distinguished and highly respected artillery officer, was the driving force behind the success of the school.

The school focused on training artillery soldiers on the use of a variety of field, siege, and seacoast guns, mortars, and howitzers. Instruction emphasized not only proper loading and firing procedures, but also the development of fuses, weights of charges, and calculating the velocities and ranges of the weapons. Officer training began on October 15, 1869, applying a theoretical approach to artillery with courses ranging from mathematics, engineering, and mechanics, to military history and law. The first graduating class was presented with diplomas by Gen. William T. Sherman. One of the more significant events that had an impact on Fort Monroe during this early-postwar period was the establishment of the "Freedmen's Bureau" by the U.S. War Department on March 3, 1865. A regional headquarters office, headed by Samuel Chapman Armstrong, was created at Fort Monroe to provide food, shelter, medical care, and education to the large contraband population, former slaves, and members of the black communities located near Fort Monroe. While the rebirth of artillery training and the work of the Freedmen's Bureau breathed new life into Fort Monroe by keeping it active in national affairs, the social scene expanded as well with the resurrection of the Hygeia Hotel. Open to the public, the first Hygeia Hotel was constructed in 1822 but was demolished in 1862 to clear an area for the fort's defense. In 1868, Henry Clark began work on the second Hygeia Hotel. However, it was not successful until 1876, when Harrison Phoebus, a prominent civilian figure, established the Hygeia as one of the best-known hotels in the world. By 1890, Fort Monroe was once again a fully functional military base, and the U.S. Army headed into a new era of weapon development.

Two soldiers and a sailor stand on the ramparts of Fort Monroe next to two 100-pounder Parrott guns sometime around 1885. At the left is a portion of the Water Battery, the fog bell, the Old Point Comfort lighthouse, the moat, and the flagstaff bastion. The Parrott guns and carriages were all removed and scrapped during the 1890s.

This undated image, probably from the early 1890s, shows the wooden bridge leading to the primary entrance ("main sallyport") to the old fort. In the background is a pedestrian bridge, and beyond that is the residence known as "the DeRussy House" and the quite extensive Hygeia Hotel. (Courtesy of Hampton University Library.)

This image shows the Old Point Comfort lighthouse, the keeper's cottage, the moat, and a bastion. Beyond the flagpole is the Hygeia Hotel, and several sailboats can be seen in the Hampton Roads harbor. This is No. 104 in a series of photographs sold to visitors by local businessman William Baulch around 1885.

After the Civil War, a "trophy park" was established on the edge of the parade ground to display stacks of cannonballs and guns going back to the Revolutionary War period. The building on the right was used to house field artillery pieces. In the background is a set of officer quarters. This is another William Baulch photograph (No. 56) from 1885.

As early as 1869, the annual Artillery School graduating class was photographed for posterity, always outdoors and usually on the parade ground. The officer seated fourth from the left is Bvt. Maj. Gen. William F. Barry, the school commandant. Barry held this position from the time when the facility reopened in 1867 until his retirement nearly 10 years later.

Here is a frontal view of Quarters No. 1, the oldest surviving residential building at Fort Monroe. Originally serving as the post engineer's quarters, it was later assigned to the commanding general until 1907. U.S. president Abraham Lincoln stayed here for nearly a week in May 1862. Many other chief executives and VIPs were entertained here. This image, complete with a horse and buggy driven by an unidentified man, dates from 1890.

Charlotte White, popularly known as "the pie woman," was a familiar figure at Fort Monroe during the late 19th century. Almost every day, she would arrive at the fort in an ox-cart filled with freshly baked pies, and she would sell them to soldiers, tourists, and other customers. It is said that P. T. Barnum gave her some money to be photographed in her cart, which initiated a new source of income for her. An extant photograph, in too poor of a condition to be reproduced in this book, does indeed depict the famous showman in White's conveyance. This 1884 image shows her with the wife and children of Maj. Gen. John C. Tidball, Artillery School commandant and post commander. In the background is the family residence, Quarters No. 1. Mabel Tidball (in the white pinafore) paid a return visit to this site in 1957.

The second Hygeia Hotel began as the Hygeia Dining Saloon in 1864. It was still a modest facility around 1873 when this image was taken, but it eventually covered a substantial piece of beachfront property. Under the shrewd management of Harrison Phoebus, the Hygeia became a popular tourist destination, but its fortunes slowly declined after his premature death in 1886.

Space has always been at a premium at Fort Monroe, as can be seen in this 1886 photograph of a small building that served as the post office as well as an oyster and lunch house operated by a Mr. Roman. A new brick post office, designed in the Romanesque Revival style and thus unlike any other building at the fort, was completed in 1898.

This "Newspaper Depot" was conveniently located near the second Hygeia Hotel at Fort Monroe. It was owned and operated by William Baulch, whose father had come here from Brooklyn, New York, during the Civil War to establish the fort's first fire department. During the 1880s, Baulch made and sold many mounted photographs of the fort. Next to this depot is an officer's residence popularly known as "the DeRussy House."

This c. 1871 photograph has been notated as a group portrait of unidentified personnel in the Fort Monroe engineer's office. All of the men are dressed in civilian attire. Of particular interest is the fact that one of these engineers is an African American, though the only significant positions open to black men at the fort were collector of customs and lighthouse keeper.

One side of the main barracks is shown in this picture, along with several warehouse buildings and a set of quarters. An unidentified artillery company is shown on dress parade, and the unit band stands farther left. This is one of the images (No. 75) made and sold by William Baulch around 1885.

This wooden structure served as the guardhouse until a new brick building was constructed in 1900. Both were located inside the moat area near the main sallyport. The image dates from 1875. A stockade containing several prison cells was located within the sallyport and survives today as a grim example of the harsh punishment meted out to soldiers who broke the rules.

Casemate 20, also known as the "First Front," was completed in 1826 as a series of gun rooms. Later it was converted to officers' quarters, as shown in this 1884 image. Across the street are several stacks of cannonballs from the Civil War era, and at the left is a Rodman gun tube. This building now serves as the home of the Casemate Museum.

CLASS OF 1884.

STRONG SLAKER GARRARD
TOWNSLEY RAFFERTY RUMBOUGH BENET GALBRAITH CATLIN STUART M^cCALLUM CUMMINS
OLIVER ROWAN BLISS LOVERIDGE
U.S. NAVY

This Artillery School graduating class is grouped around an artillery limber and includes a naval officer. Standing directly in front of the right wheel is the school adjutant, Tasker H. Bliss, who was later the U.S. Army chief of staff during World War I. Bliss was one of the few artillery officers ever to achieve such an important appointment.

Fort Monroe's Protestant church is called the Chapel of the Centurion after Cornelius, who is said to be the first Roman soldier to convert to Christianity. It was located inside the moat area and was dedicated in May 1858. This 1884 photograph was taken by William Baulch. The wooden sets of officer quarters to the right of the church were new at the time, and all are still standing.

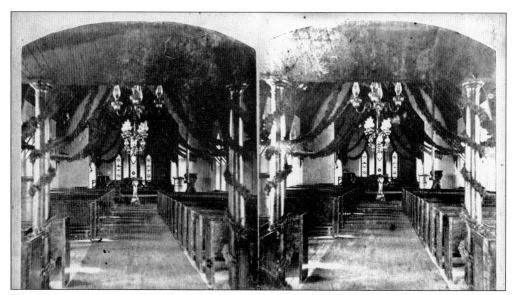

Here is a rare interior view of the post chapel from around 1875, apparently at Christmas time. This image comes from a stereograph published by an unidentified manufacturer. Note the stove at the right side and the baptismal font in front of the altar (a reminder that this church's first chaplain was an Episcopalian minister).

This ghostly image depicts the officer's residence known as "the DeRussy House," and the two ladies might be members of the DeRussy family. Rene DeRussy served as the post engineer and post commander at Fort Monroe during his long military career. At the time of his death in November 1865, Brigadier General DeRussy was the oldest West Point graduate on active duty. According to custom, his much younger widow was expected to quickly vacate her quarters at Fort Monroe. However, Helen Augusta DeRussy had other ideas and decided to remain indefinitely. This led to a potentially embarrassing situation for the fort, which needed the space for new arrivals but was reluctant to evict the widow of a distinguished army officer. She left the premises in November 1891 and moved to New York. Every structure in this photograph was demolished during the construction boom from 1907 to 1912.

This image by William Baulch (No. 105) depicts officer quarters and casemates inside the moat area around 1885. At right are the entrances to the First Front (now Building 20), and at the end of the road is the Second Front (Building 21). At the left is Building 19. The twin sets of quarters, once unofficially known as "the Tuilieries," are Buildings 18 and 17, followed by Building 16. (Courtesy of Hampton University Library.)

This rare stereographic image from 1880 or earlier depicts an unidentified man in a wheelchair sitting on the edge of the parade ground. In the background is the post headquarters of that era, long before the present building was constructed in 1894. Prior to the 1890s, most army buildings on post were located within the moat area, except for the arsenal.

Two

MODERNIZING
FORT MONROE
1891–1916

The last decades of the 19th century introduced many technological improvements that gave new strength to U.S. coastal defenses. The age of smoothbore cannons ended, with much of Fort Monroe's arsenal becoming unsuited for modern warfare. With the development of steel breech-loading disappearing guns, 12-inch mortars, and 3- and 6-inch rapid-fire barbette guns, Fort Monroe became the center of a formidable defense system. In 1907, the U.S. Army's Artillery Corps was officially separated into two branches, Coast Artillery Corps and Field Artillery Corps. The Field Artillery Corps moved with its own school to Fort Sill, Oklahoma, while Fort Monroe became the headquarters for the new Coast Artillery School. Within the next few years, a massive construction program was instituted to create a new campus near the Hotel Chamberlin. Fort Monroe's success in rapidly constructing new buildings was due to the addition of a railroad extending from the town of Phoebus over Mill Creek. In June 1890, the Chesapeake and Ohio Railway (C&O) began operating, allowing rail cars to carry food, fuel, and supplies. The railroad also provided transportation for gunpowder and ammunition for the new coast defense weapons. For measuring distances along this railroad, Fort Monroe was designated as "Mile Post Zero." To distribute military supplies to the defense batteries along Fort Monroe's coast, an army-operated railroad was constructed in 1897 to meet the C&O line at the front gate. Continuing the success of the Hygeia hotels, the Hotel Chamberlin opened in April 1896 and became the social center of Fort Monroe, attracting tourists from around the world. Extending the religious services on Fort Monroe, a Roman Catholic church, St. Mary Star-of-the-Sea, originally built in 1860, was replaced with a new structure in 1903. In the same year, the U.S. Army YMCA was opened, expanding activities for soldiers and their families. During this time, Fort Monroe was a bustling army post with new technology shaping its layout and mission. The Coast Artillery School proved to be Fort Monroe's most important mission, and the extensive training American soldiers received there would prepare them for the challenges of World War I.

This image from 1900 of Fort Monroe's moat shows a portion of the Water Battery, the Old Point Comfort lighthouse, and the flagstaff bastion. In the background is the massive Hygeia Hotel, and just beyond it is the Hotel Chamberlin. For a brief period, these two resort hotels operated as rivals and then as partners owned by the same corporation. This is one of many shots of Fort Monroe by C. E. Cheyne, a prominent local photographer.

The Water Battery, Fort Monroe's oldest structure for gun emplacements outside the moat, was situated in front of the East Gate. By the beginning of the 20th century, its Rodman guns were completely obsolete, so a regrettable decision was made to demolish the battery in 1907. Today only a portion of the powder magazine survives.

This picturesque winter scene was taken on January 29, 1899, from the roof of the Hygeia Hotel. The wooden porch along the flagstaff bastion was part of the Fort Monroe Officers' Club, unofficially known as the "Casemate Club." Just beyond the moat was the Water Battery. The road along the right side led past the fog bell tower and the lighthouse.

This photograph of the trophy park section of the parade ground depicts two soldiers, several benches, and many live oak trees. In the background are the post chapel and Quarters 15, still in use today. A notation on the back states, "F.C.P. Jollifle. Fortress Monroe, Va. April 15 – 1900. Easter."

The Fort Monroe gun yard was located on land across from the Hotel Chamberlin and was later occupied by Coast Artillery School buildings. This image from the late 1890s shows newly scrapped iron gun carriages, as well as Parrott and Rodman gun tubes. In the center background is William Baulch's tobacco and souvenir store.

Battery Parrott, named for ordnance expert Robert Parrott, was activated in 1906. It held two Model 1900 twelve-inch disappearing guns, the most powerful weapons ever placed at Fort Monroe. This photograph of one of these guns in action was taken around 1915. Battery Parrott was a coast defense showcase for many years.

Gun crew members are shown with two 12-inch seacoast mortars in one of the mortar pits at Battery Anderson. Part of a third gun can be seen near the upper right side of the photograph, taken around 1913. These weapons were once major components of American coast defense installations, but today they can only be seen at Fort DeSoto in St. Petersburg, Florida.

In 1907, the Artillery Corps split into two branches, the Coast Artillery Corps and the Field Artillery Corps. The Artillery School at Fort Monroe became the Coast Artillery School, and a new set of buildings was constructed. Shown here is Murray Hall (Building 133) and, behind it, Lewis Hall (Building 134). Both were completed in 1909, when this photograph was taken. Note the streetcar tracks and brick pavement in the road.

Many social organizations have existed at Fort Monroe, but most have come and gone without leaving adequate documentation. This group photograph by C. E. Cheyne is the only source of information about the glee club, which consisted of four tenors and four basses. The image is undated but probably comes from the early 1900s.

Army bands have been important sources of morale support and entertainment at Fort Monroe since the 1820s, when Col. Abraham Eustis requested that musicians be sent here. This is a group shot of the 4th Band, Artillery Corps, around 1903. Drum major Ira J. Wharton is seated to the left of the two drums.

The 4th Army Band parades along Fort Monroe's main street, now known as Ingalls Road, around 1906. Behind the group is the first Hotel Chamberlin, a popular resort hotel of the day. In front of the hotel is the Old Point–Buckroe Beach streetcar in the distance, and barely seen is an Old Bay Line steamship providing passenger service to Baltimore.

In this unusual scene, a boatload of U. S. Marines lands at Old Point Comfort, undoubtedly from a naval vessel anchored in Hampton Roads. At left is the newly built Hotel Chamberlin, and on the right is a portion of the older Hygeia Hotel. The smaller buildings between the hotels are business establishments. Note the streetcar stopping to take on passengers. This postcard image probably dates from about 1901.

The U.S. Army YMCA at Fort Monroe opened in 1903, thanks in large measure to the generosity of Helen Gould, daughter of the controversial financier Jay Gould. It was an important center of social and athletic activities for nine decades. The YMCA gradually closed all of its operations on military posts, and the Fort Monroe facility was the last one to go.

The U.S. Army YMCA provided classrooms, a movie theater, reading rooms, and various activities to boost troop morale. In this posed image from about 1910, soldiers are making use of the gymnasium equipment. After this facility closed in 1992, it underwent substantial renovation before reopening as a physical fitness center.

A brave photographer stood on the roof of the Hotel Chamberlin to capture this view of the rival Hygeia Hotel and the Fort Monroe waterfront. The image dates from approximately 1899, during a brief period when two resort hotels and the Sherwood Inn flourished at the fort. The Hygeia was demolished in 1902, and the site is now known as Continental Park.

During the early 1900s, the Hotel Chamberlin at Fort Monroe became a popular tourist destination, playing host to composers John Philip Sousa and Charles Ives, actress Mabel Normand, financier J. P. Morgan, and many other notables. To the right of the hotel is one of the newly completed Coast Artillery School buildings. (Courtesy of Mariners' Museum.)

This photograph from about 1908 depicts the old and the new at Fort Monroe. In contrast to the horse and buggy are the newly constructed sets of officer quarters along the street now known as Fenwick Road. The imposing building with the white columns has served as the commanding general's residence since 1918.

A crowd gathers to watch Fort Monroe troops boarding the U.S. Army transport *Kilpatrick* on March 11, 1911. The 6th, 35th, 41st, 69th, and 73rd Companies of the Coast Artillery Corps were ordered to Galveston, Texas, in response to revolutionary activity in Mexico. These troops became part of the 2nd Provisional Regiment at Fort Crockett but saw no action before returning home on July 10, 1911.

First Lt. Moses Robert Ross bears the sad distinction of being the only officer known to drown in Fort Monroe's moat. He served in the Spanish-American War and the Philippine Insurrection before joining the Coast Artillery Corps. Ross arrived at Fort Monroe from Fort Adams, Rhode Island, on May 1, 1905, with the 79th Company to participate in joint army-navy maneuvers. Early on the morning of May 6, Ross left the Officers' Club, mounted a bicycle borrowed from a friend, and was never seen alive again. Later that day, the 26-year-old man's body was recovered from the moat and was shipped home to Washington, Pennsylvania. It is believed that the chain of his bicycle snapped suddenly, pitching Ross over the handlebars and head first into the shallow water. Many years later, his younger brother, Rear Adm. Richard Ross of the U.S. Coast Guard, donated the unfortunate victim's uniforms and other personal belongings to the Casemate Museum.

The above picture shows the men who were actually in the gun pit at the time of the accident at Fort Monroe, July 21, 1910. Those with a * before their names were killed. No. 1 Robinson, 2 Thomas, 3 Davenport, 4 *Duffy, 5 Hoffman, 6 Raney, 7 Summer, 8 *Smith, 9 Gleason, 10 Humphreys, 11 *Sullivan, 12 Kennedy, 13 Sulzberger, 14 Newsom, 15 *Allie, 16 *Chadwick, 17 Brinkley, 18 *K. 19 *Hogan, 20 *Hess, 21 *Bradford, 22 *Turner, 23 Clement. Atkins killed, not in picture.

Fort Monroe's most tragic accident occurred on July 21, 1910, at Battery DeRussy during a firing demonstration. A 12-inch disappearing gun was fired before its breechblock could be closed, causing a terrible explosion that killed 11 members of the gun crew. This disaster was witnessed by the chief of coast artillery and the chief of ordnance. This photograph shows the men who were in the gun pit at that time.

On July 22, 1910, a memorial service for the gun accident victims drew a large turnout from Fort Monroe personnel and the local civilian community. The remains of the 11 soldiers were then transported by horse-drawn caissons from the parade ground to the Chesapeake and Ohio Railway station on post for shipment to their families.

32

Here is a formal photograph of a crew with a disappearing gun. This weapon received its name because of the unique hydraulic carriage that raised and then lowered the gun during a firing operation. The men wore brown work uniforms that were later replaced by the more familiar blue denim outfits. This image dates from about 1910.

Four crew members pose with a 12-inch mortar at Battery Anderson. Four of these weapons were installed in each of the two gun pits that comprised the battery. During World War I, two mortars were permanently removed from each pit. Seacoast mortars were designed to send projectiles in an arching pattern onto the vulnerable decks of warships.

Officers and several enlisted men are shown beside two of the 3-inch rapid-fire guns at Battery Irwin around 1915. The armament was removed from these gun pits after World War I. Barely visible in the upper left portion are the steamship wharf and the Hotel Chamberlin. On the right is the lighthouse keeper's cottage.

The blanket toss was a favorite bivouac pastime during the early 1900s, when this image was made. It was considered a rite of passage for any rookie in the unit. The site is one of Fort Monroe's "disappearing" gun batteries, possibly Battery Church. During regularly scheduled periods each year, Coast Artillery Corps companies moved from their permanent barracks to campgrounds near the batteries for intensive training.

This view of Ingalls Road, Fort Monroe's main street, dates from 1907. The large building to the left of the streetcar is the Sherwood Inn, and on the right is St. Mary Star-of-the-Sea Catholic Church, constructed in 1903 to replace a wooden building that had served the local Catholic community since 1860.

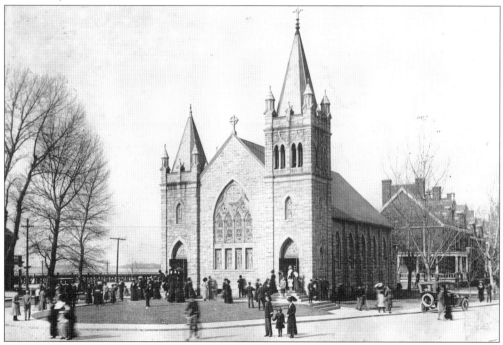

Roman Catholics at Fort Monroe received permission to establish their own house of worship in 1860, just two years after a permanent Protestant church was completed. In 1903, the original St. Mary Star-of-the-Sea church building was replaced by this much more imposing structure. The two steeples have since been removed.

Members of the 73rd Company, Coast Artillery Corps, line up for inspection in front of Building 5, the largest set of barracks within the moat area. Note the towels and other laundry items draped over the balcony railings. This unit was stationed at Fort Monroe from February 1901 to April 1916, when it was transferred to the Panama Canal Zone.

U.S. Army regulars enjoy a meal in front of the Hotel Chamberlin in May 1898 before heading off to Cuba to fight in the Spanish-American War. Fort Monroe became a major treatment center for sick and wounded soldiers during the war. One of the hospital ships that stopped here brought back newspaper correspondent Stephen Crane.

Two enlisted men pose beside a 12-pounder howitzer from the Civil War era, possibly the same one now on display at the Casemate Museum. In the background is Building 10, a set of company barracks now used as offices. This postcard is undated but is probably from around 1910.

Intramural and interservice athletic contests have been held at Fort Monroe since at least the late 19th century. This football game on an extremely muddy field (actually, the parade ground) was played between a post team and a visiting navy team, judging by the many sailors in the crowd. It dates from about 1910.

Coast Artillery Corps companies at Fort Monroe fielded their own sports teams in intramural competition. Here is the 169th Company's baseball team with its officer sponsor and young mascot, who is likely the officer's son, around 1911. This image was donated to the Casemate Museum by Lt. Col. John Esper Jr., whose father was stationed here at that time.

This postcard image depicts a typical artillery company mess room, probably located in Building 5. The card is postmarked January 15, 1907, which accords with the two 45-star flags on the wall. Oklahoma became the 46th state in November 1907. This item was sent to Mrs. Bessie Richard in Spencer, West Virginia, with a message asking, "Dear Bes why dont you rite."

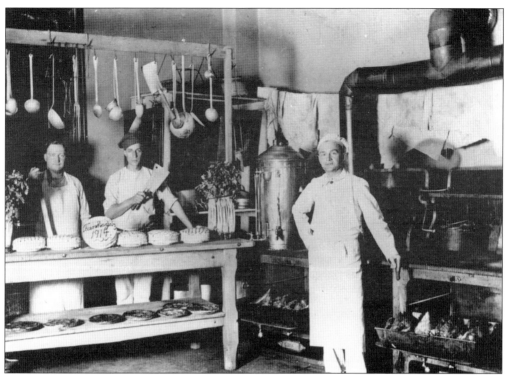

An unidentified chef and two assistants pose with their turkeys, pies, and cakes for a Thanksgiving dinner on November 26, 1914. This might be the Fort Monroe Officers' (Casemate) Club kitchen, but it looks more like a mess kitchen in one of the enlisted barracks at Buildings 5 or 10.

The all-important army cooks and other kitchen personnel are shown in front of the outdoor mess facility during a scheduled encampment at Battery Anderson or Ruggles in this c. 1915 photograph. These men were not necessarily assigned to a Fort Monroe company since units from other installations sometimes trained here.

A porch around the Fort Monroe Officers' (Casemate) Club was authorized in 1894, and patrons could reach it by a flat-bottom boat affectionately dubbed, "the Maid of the Moat." In this photograph from about 1916, an unidentified club employee demonstrates the method of propelling this craft across the water.

This unidentified young woman, probably an officer's daughter, appears to know what she is doing as she takes aim at the Fort Monroe rifle range. The image dates from the early 1900s and is not quite as unusual as one might think. Female sharpshooters such as Annie Oakley had already captured the public's fancy.

An unidentified enlisted man in the Medical Corps poses with a female relative or friend dressed in one of his spare uniforms. They are standing on the ramparts next to a 12-pounder howitzer from the Civil War era. At that time, Fort Monroe possessed many such relics dating back as far as the Revolutionary War, but scrap drives and donations to various historical sites gradually reduced this collection to approximately two dozen guns.

These two ladies are Margaret and Emma Grady from nearby Phoebus. They are shown with a Civil War-era Rodman gun in Cannon Park, across the road from post headquarters. This snapshot dates from around 1916. The gun is still on display at the same location.

Photographs of Fort Monroe's enlisted men and their families from the early 1900s are rare. Among those pictured here is Brigid Rassmussen, the wife of electrical sergeant Christian Rassmussen, who is sitting on the top step at the right. Across from her, on the same step, is her son James and just below her, is her son Stephen. The girl with the hair ribbon is Margaret King, a neighbor's child. The three women on the porch might be Brigid's relatives. This was taken at Quarters 130 (22 and 24 Tidball Street) in 1913. The building is still in use as noncommissioned officer housing. This picture is part of a collection of Rassmussen images discovered by the new owners of a house in the Phoebus section of Hampton, Virginia, in 1993. Included were several postcards from Denmark, Christian Rassmussen's native country.

Fort Monroe's troop-carrying train arrives from camp at the ordnance storehouse near the North Gate, around 1910. This structure, now known as Building 135, was completed in 1908 and has been used for many purposes since then. The letters on the car stand for United States Quarter Master Department.

During the Coast Artillery Corps era, Fort Monroe maintained its own railroad line to transport troops and supplies to the various gun batteries located along the route that is now known as Fenwick Road. This particular artillery company camp was set up across from Battery Parrott. The brick building in the background with the arched entrance was the post engineer's office.

This unidentified young lady might be anticipating a romantic rendezvous in the Hotel Chamberlin's dance pavilion overlooking the harbor. Note the vessels barely visible in the background. The photograph was probably taken around 1910. The Chamberlin was a popular place for unattached women to meet bachelor officers, and its management even advertised this fact.

Two officers with an unidentified artillery company are shown in bivouac at Battery Anderson around 1915. This unit would have spent several months each year in camp at this site to undergo training with 12-inch seacoast mortars. Training with various types of seacoast weapons was a key element in Fort Monroe's mission.

Three

FORT MONROE IN THE GREAT WAR
1917–1919

In April 1917, America entered World War I and launched a program to transform a small peacetime army into a large fighting force. The war also created an urgent need for officers. As a consequence, the Coast Artillery School at Fort Monroe terminated its academic term early and gave way to the Coast Artillery Training Center for the duration of the war. The center immediately began training officer candidates and enlisted men. This new program also included, for the first time, a five-week course on antiaircraft artillery, as well as classes on clerical, electrical, radio, and motor transportation fields. The total number of graduates from the training center was 4,400 officers and 4,200 enlisted men. The army's first school for chaplains was initiated at Fort Monroe in March 1918, though it only graduated one class before moving to another post. To handle the influx of military personnel, Fort Monroe began to expand its facilities. By 1918, more than 250 buildings were constructed all over Fort Monroe, including section rooms, barracks, quarters, latrines, warehouses, and gun sheds. However, this new construction was not enough to quell the crowded conditions. The army began filling the shores of Mill Creek, establishing bulkheads where additional buildings were subsequently placed. The end of the war ceased all activity, and the process of demobilization began at Fort Monroe. The Coast Artillery School returned to its normal class schedules, though the training center continued until 1923. In December 1919, units started mustering out of Fort Monroe, and once again the installation returned to peace status.

This stereograph image depicts some of the 1,200 officer candidates at the first Coast Artillery Training Camp, which began on June 18, 1917. They are shown marching on Fort Monroe's parade ground. When the camp closed, 766 men received commissions on August 15. A second training camp for 1,277 candidates operated from September 22 to November 26, granting commissions to 818 men. By this time, an alternate program at Fort Winfield Scott, California, was discontinued, and all the Coast Artillery Corps training during the remainder of the war took place at Fort Monroe. The third camp (occurring from January 5 to March 26, 1918,) suffered through unusually cold weather and only commissioned 447 second lieutenants, but the fourth camp (from April 6 to June 26) did not fare much better, with 467 commissions. The camp schedules were then modified until the end of the war, by which time more than 4,400 officers and 4,200 enlisted men had completed their training at Fort Monroe.

Here is a rare image of officer candidates at a Fort Monroe mortar battery on June 26, 1917, during the first U.S. Coast Artillery Training Camp. Considering that thousands of men attended these camps, few photographs of this type have come to light. This is from a set of snapshots donated to the Casemate Museum in 1961 by Byron Cecil.

Here is a view of a classroom in the Enlisted Men's Division of the Coast Artillery School. A notation on the back reads, "Our class room, where I spend so many hours. On the right of the picture, the second chair you see is mine and that is where I sit always when I write to you. That's where I am writing this now."

This publicity photograph is captioned, "Making the World Safe for Democracy—Our Boys Training for the Firing Line, Ft. Monroe, Va. – 1917." The instructor is probably an infantry officer. Such training was part of the curriculum for Coast Artillery Corps soldiers during the war, though few, if any, would ever fire a rifle in battle.

This companion image is titled, "Mess Time Out on the Rifle Range of a Southern Cantonment, Fort Monroe, Va. – 1917." A note on the back of the image states, "A typical daily ration consisted of 18 oz. bread, ½ oz. butter or 1.28 oz. jam, 20 oz. potatoes, 12 oz. bacon, 24 oz. beans, .64 oz. lard, .64 oz. salt, .04 oz. pepper, .17 gill vinegar, 1.12 oz. coffee, 3.2 oz. sugar, 5 oz. evaporated milk."

Coast Artillery Corps officers and enlisted men conduct a training exercise with 3-inch, balanced, pillar, rapid-fire guns at Battery Irwin during World War I. Construction on this battery had begun in 1900, but its guns were removed after the war ended. Today two of the gun pits hold 3-inch guns salvaged from Battery Lee at nearby Fort Wool in May of 1947.

Coast Artillery Corps officers or officer candidates conduct a surveying exercise on the edge of the parade ground during World War I. A 15-inch Rodman cannon, known as "the Lincoln gun," can be seen on the left. Ruckman Road, with its sets of officer quarters dating from the 1880s, is in the background.

Here is a parking lot for heavy-duty tractors, trucks, and armored personnel carriers at Fort Monroe in 1918. The enlisted quarters in the background are still in use. Considering the scarcity of housing on the post at that time, it is remarkable that so much space was allotted to these vehicles.

Three heavy-duty military tractors make their way across the shallow end of Mill Creek just outside Fort Monroe in 1918. These tractors were designed to transport field guns nicknamed "Long Toms," which enjoyed a brief vogue in the coast artillery arsenal but were phased out over the next few years.

An unidentified U.S. Coast Artilleryman poses on the Fort Monroe mine dock with a variety of submarine mine buoys. On the left is the aft portion of an army mine planter, probably the *Gen. Samuel M. Mills.* This submarine mine program was significant throughout the Coast Artillery Corps era.

Pictures of army mine planters are hardly scarce, but images of support vessels are less common. Here are three crewmen in a distribution box boat near Fort Monroe. Their job was to attach cables from a mine to a cast-iron case with other cables running to a mine casemate on shore. The case and mine were then anchored to the sea floor.

This U.S. Army YMCA classroom is apparently being used to tutor soldiers in basic mathematics during World War I. Note the civilian instructor standing near one of the blackboards. The YMCA program at Fort Monroe began in 1889 in temporary facilities and continued until 1992, when the parent organization decided to terminate its relationship with the fort.

This Signal Corps photograph depicts a drafting class at the Coast Artillery School, undated but possibly from World War I. This was only one of many highly technical subjects taught at the school during its four decades of operation at Fort Monroe. The Coast Artillery Corps was perhaps the most technology-oriented branch of the U.S. Army, but, ironically, advances in technology led to its downfall.

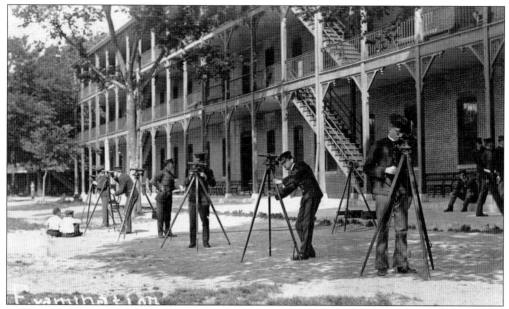

Officer candidates at a Coast Artillery Corps training camp are examined on their knowledge of the transit, a surveying instrument also used to plot gun positions. The officer holding a set of papers is undoubtedly the class instructor. Two small boys are intently watching this exercise taking place in front of a barracks building in 1917 or 1918.

This aerial view of a portion of the Fort Monroe waterfront depicts the steamship wharf at lower right, the Hotel Chamberlin and its attached dance pavilion at center, and the Coast Artillery School campus behind the hotel. The large building at upper left, near the St. Mary Star-of-the-Sea Church, is the Sherwood Inn.

These young officers and officer candidates are doing some fireside reading in the main lobby of the Fort Monroe YMCA in this *c.* 1918 photograph. The man on the far left appears to be perusing a movie fan magazine, while the soldier third from left is reading a local newspaper, the *Norfolk Public Ledger.* For these men, the Fort Monroe YMCA was probably their favorite place to relax and socialize while attending the officers' training camp. Many YMCA facilities on military bases were in operation during the first half of the 20th century, but they were gradually phased out. In 1992, the YMCA decided to close its Fort Monroe branch and donated it to the army. After a considerable amount of renovation, the building was reopened as a physical fitness center. This particular photograph made it possible to restore the fireplace and mantle to their original appearance.

This 15-inch Rodman cannon, known as "the Lincoln gun," has been displayed at the edge of the parade ground for many decades. It bears the serial number "1," and its nickname is a tribute to Abraham Lincoln's interest in weaponry. Standing next to the gun is Capt. Ralph D. Horn, and sitting above the muzzle is Ralph Horn Jr. The image is dated 1917.

Three women and a dog stand on the edge of the parade ground on a winter day around 1918. In the background is a 15-inch Rodman gun from the Civil War, as well as Quarters No. 62, a duplex structure for officers' families. The gun and the quarters are still in place, along with most of the live oaks in this image. (Courtesy of the Hampton History Museum.)

An elderly African American identified only as "Uncle Lewis" stands near one of Fort Monroe's four bridges across the moat. Southern whites often addressed older black men of their acquaintance as "Uncle," an affectionate greeting that is now sometimes considered demeaning and insensitive. This image dates from World War I, and the man might have been born into slavery. (Courtesy of the Hampton History Museum.)

An unidentified enlisted man stands in front of Building 142 and its twin, Building 141, which are known as "the Flattops" because of their flat roofs. These residences facing Hampton Roads were colonels' quarters during the war but were later reserved for general officers. Note the stripes near the man's left cuff.

A vocal quartet performs for a mixed audience of mess cooks, several officers, their dependents, and a family dog in the Wilson Park area of Fort Monroe around 1918. One can easily imagine this group singing "Keep the Home Fires Burning" or some other wartime favorite in an era prior to the advent of Bob Hope and USO shows.

A Coast Artillery Corps officer is presenting a song or recitation for his comrades, several civilians, and a group of interested children near the Wilson Park firing range during World War I. Fort Monroe did not even have a theater at that time, so entertainment venues were quite makeshift and oriented toward amateurs.

The four secretaries at the Fort Monroe YMCA pose in their uniforms around 1918. These women would have been busy dealing with the thousands of officers and soldiers who went through the fort during World War I. Unfortunately, their names are not known. (Courtesy of the Hampton History Museum.)

Newly commissioned officers in the Coast Artillery Corps march across Fort Monroe's main sallyport bridge during World War I. The third training camp began on January 5, 1918, with 613 candidates and was hampered by severely cold weather. It ended on March 26, when 447 commissions were issued. Two additional camps were in operation between April and September, and then a "continuous camp" was in effect until the demobilization period.

Four

CHALLENGES
1920–1940

Many challenges faced the leadership of Fort Monroe at the end of World War I. With the reduction of troops, outdated equipment, and budget cuts, the U.S. Army was in a period of decline. The lethargy of peacetime activities permeated Fort Monroe but eventually subsided because of the new missions it acquired. By 1926, Fort Monroe became the hub of all U.S. Coast Artillery programs, including the Third Coast Artillery District, the Harbor Defense of Chesapeake Bay, and the Coast Artillery Board. Despite the new missions it acquired, Fort Monroe was tremendously impacted by the Great Depression of the early 1930s. The Coast Artillery School's budget was significantly decreased, with the resulting loss of 60 percent of its staff and faculty. Standard seacoast artillery training continued at Fort Monroe, but with the advancement of airplanes, the mission of the Coast Artillery School was drastically altered to focus on antiaircraft artillery. Even limited by budget cutbacks, the entire program was revised with more courses being offered on this new technology. In 1932, improvement in submarine mining also led to new curriculum at the Submarine Mine Depot on Fort Monroe. To help combat America's financial crisis, Fort Monroe played an important role in the Civilian Conservation Corps (CCC). In 1933, Fort Monroe processed more than 5,000 enrollees, who worked all over the United States. Two CCC camps for African American men were established within the fort itself. Fort Monroe also suffered through its share of disasters. On March 7, 1920, the Hotel Chamberlin caught fire and burned to the ground, bringing an end to the popular tourist destination. In the evening of August 22, 1933, a major hurricane hit Fort Monroe and the Hampton Roads area.

The rebuilding of Fort Monroe coincided with the U.S. government's massive spending plan to counteract the Great Depression in 1934. The post–World War I era held many challenges for Fort Monroe, but in the end, the post fought through and remained an important training center for the army. By 1939, a new threat appeared with Germany's invasion of Poland, and by 1941, America would find itself in another world war.

The Moat - Officers' Club Entrance, Ft. Monroe, Va.

This view includes a radio tower, the moat, the flagstaff bastion, and, in the distance, the second Hotel Chamberlin prior to World War II. This was a period of tremendous construction activity at Fort Monroe, spurred by the Great Depression and war threats, though one would never realize that from this tranquil scene.

This winter scene from around 1920 shows the government pier in the foreground, the seawall, a row of general officer quarters, and a bandstand that survived the demolition of the Hygeia Hotel. This structure continued to be used for outdoor concerts until it was destroyed by a hurricane in August 1933.

On May 24, 1924, the 100th anniversary of the Artillery School (now called the Coast Artillery School) was celebrated at Fort Monroe. The dignitaries included Gen. John J. Pershing (first row, center) and Virginia governor E. Lee Trinkle (first row, holding hat). This was one of General Pershing's final public appearances in uniform before he retired from military service.

A group of Reserve Officers' Training Corps (ROTC) cadets is given training with the 3-inch antiaircraft gun at Wilson Park in June 1938. During World War II, this weapon was replaced by the much more effective 90-millimeter antiaircraft gun. Summer camps for ROTC students began at Fort Monroe as early as 1919 and continued through 1941.

Members of Battery D, 52nd Coast Artillery Regiment, prepare to load a practice round into a 12-inch railway mortar. This exercise at Fort Monroe on April 15, 1938, demonstrates the importance of railway artillery after World War I at American coast defense installations.

This image gives some idea of the huge amount of munitions required by a coast defense post such as Fort Monroe during the early 20th century. Here are rows of 12-inch mortar projectiles on display at either Battery Anderson or Battery Ruggles around 1925. The light colored rounds (in the foreground) are 700-pound projectiles, while the dark ones with caps (barely visible in the background) are M1907 deck-piercing rounds.

The gun crew of an unknown unit poses in front of a Fort Monroe battery, possibly Battery Church, during the 1920s. Note the disappearing gun with its breechblock covered behind the railing. These batteries were always popular with photographers, even during World War II when, presumably, cameras were prohibited.

In this companion photograph, an enlisted man is shown near the gun pit of the same battery pictured above. To the left is an ammunition cart with a projectile ready to be loaded. Working in these pits was especially uncomfortable in hot, humid weather because there was absolutely no shade.

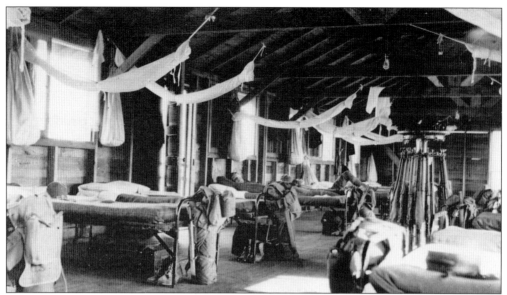

During the interwar period, Fort Monroe provided summer training for West Point cadets, the Virginia National Guard, ROTC students, and participants in the Civilian Military Training Camp (CMTC) program. Here is a rare view of the interior of a ROTC barracks in July 1923. The hanging sheets would be rolled down at night to provide some privacy. Note that two of the cots are occupied.

This German railway gun was captured during World War I and was shipped to Fort Monroe as a trophy. It was placed in front of the Liberty Theatre in 1920 and stood there until 1942, when it was cut up for wartime scrap metal. Another German gun was displayed near the hospital and met the same fate.

The U.S. Army Mine Planter Service was an important component of Fort Monroe's defense mission from about 1909 to 1946. This Signal Corps photograph depicts the mine planter *Gen. William M. Graham* undergoing a sea trial in September 1931 after being reconditioned at the fort.

Four U.S. Army crewmen in blue denim work uniforms prepare to lower a buoy and submarine mine from the deck of an unidentified mine planter off Fort Monroe in April 1933. Because of its harbor defense mission, the Coast Artillery Corps, rather than the navy, was given the task of submarine mining.

The Hotel Chamberlin was a popular tourist destination and a center of social activities at Fort Monroe from the time it opened in April 1896. Unfortunately, it was also a firetrap. On March 7, 1920, fire broke out in the laundry room, possibly due to faulty electrical wiring. The blaze spread quickly, and smoke began to pour from the building, as shown in this image.

This view of the left side of the Chamberlin, expresses much better than words the magnitude of the fire. Miraculously, no deaths or serious injuries were reported, but the destruction of the hotel left a gaping hole in Fort Monroe's social scene that would not be filled for another eight years.

The complete destruction of the Hotel Chamberlin and adjacent buildings is shown in this snapshot, perhaps taken from the roof of the news depot at the nearby steamship wharf on March 8, 1920. The remaining brick structures were quickly knocked down, and the lot was completely cleared. It remained empty until a second Hotel Chamberlin was begun in 1927.

This 1925 aerial view of Fort Monroe shows the installation without a resort hotel. The vacant land on the left is the site of the first Hotel Chamberlin after the fire in 1920. The parkland across the road was occupied by the second Hygeia Hotel until it was demolished in 1902. The Old Point–Buckroe Beach streetcar can be seen heading for the wharf where the Old Bay Line offered passenger service to Baltimore.

During the night of August 22, 1933, a major storm struck Fort Monroe, causing millions of dollars of damage to buildings, artillery weapons, equipment, and a railroad trestle. Severe flooding continued during the next day, as shown in this photograph of pedestrians crossing the main sallyport bridge. Remarkably, no deaths or serious injuries occurred at the fort.

As a result of the August 1933 storm damage, Fort Monroe began a massive construction and renovation program, including a new seawall. The highlights of this program are depicted here. Credit for much of this work should go to the post adjutant, Maj. Harrington Cochran, who was also an early advocate of a bridge-tunnel between Norfolk and Hampton.

The second Hotel Chamberlin opened in April 1928 and undoubtedly would have become as successful as its predecessor had it not been for the Great Depression and World War II. This July 1938 photograph was taken from the deck of the ferryboat that made daily trips between Old Point Comfort and Norfolk. The hotel's imposing twin domes were removed, robbing the exterior of its most notable feature, shortly after the United States entered the war.

Bill, the Hotel Chamberlin driver who transported guests to and from the train station and other places, was ready and waiting for a passenger in this 1939 photograph. He could not have known that rail service to Fort Monroe would end after November 1939, and in 1942, the U. S. Navy would take over the hotel.

On July 29, 1940, U.S. president Franklin D. Roosevelt visited Fort Monroe as part of a tour of military installations. The president arrived at the steamship wharf next to the Hotel Chamberlin, met with area military commanders, and observed a firing demonstration at Wilson Park. In this photograph, Roosevelt and members of his party render honors to the flag while the national anthem is played.

Artillerymen prepare for a firing demonstration with a 3-inch antiaircraft gun at Wilson Park in November 1934. Because of Fort Monroe's significance as a training facility, these exercises were fairly common. Wilson Park was distant enough from offices and quarters that broken windows were not a problem.

Crewmen are shown with one of Battery Montgomery's two 6-inch rapid-fire guns in June 1938. This was the last of Fort Monroe's major concrete batteries to be installed, and in March 1948, it became the last one to be taken out of service, effectively ending the fort's connection with Coast Artillery Corps activities.

Newly commissioned officers in the U.S. Army Reserve examine an M3 gun director at Wilson Park in June 1938. A training film from that period demonstrates that this gun director was an extremely complicated piece of equipment that required highly skilled personnel to operate it properly.

Because of their importance in World War I, railway guns were quickly adopted into the coastal defense arsenal. In this image, members of Battery F, 51st Coast Artillery Regiment, prepare an 8-inch railway gun for firing. The stabilizers keep the flatcar in place during this operation. This is one of a series of training shots taken on April 15, 1938.

The Officers' Beach Club was constructed in 1932, and an outdoor swimming pool was added two years later. In the background are the 12-inch mortar pits of Batteries Ruggles and Anderson. Not viewable in this photograph was a nine-hole golf course that was completely destroyed by a 1933 hurricane and was never rebuilt.

The Chamberlin's outdoor pool facing Hampton Roads harbor was a popular place on the day this photograph was taken. The vehicles parked on the wharf indicate a date in the late 1930s. The hotel's relations with Fort Monroe were quite strained at times, especially when management briefly installed slot machines.

A Fort Monroe basketball team from the early 1930s poses with its managers and officer coach on the steps of the Fort Monroe YMCA building. Sports activities have become increasingly important at military installations for their contribution to team building, physical fitness, and entertainment.

The post chapel, known as the Chapel of the Centurion, is shown in a postcard from about 1940. During that period, it was painted green with red trim, in accordance with army specifications. Later, to everyone's relief, the building was restored to its pristine white appearance.

A group of young people is on its way to first communion at St. Mary Star-of-the-Sea Catholic Church in the 1920s. A priest is barely visible standing between the 7th and 8th girl from the left. As the only Catholic church within miles, St. Mary had a large and active congregation at that time.

The wartime need to provide entertainment for troops through commercial films and stage productions led to the construction of "Liberty Theatres" at many U.S. Army posts. This particular building did not open until March 1920, sixteen months after the Armistice. It was located at the end of present-day Reeder Circle and was demolished in 1938 after the Fort Monroe Theatre was completed.

After the "Maid of the Moat" was retired, a wooden bridge was constructed over the moat to the Fort Monroe Officers' Club. The water is not visible in this 1920s image, but the garrison flag is prominently displayed. Also pictured are a boy in a sailor suit and a female relative sitting behind him.

The Sherwood Inn was initially a cottage built in 1843 by post sutler Dr. Robert Archer. In 1867, Mrs. S. F. Eaton acquired the property and operated it as a boardinghouse for 20 years, gradually enlarging the inn until it could accommodate 175 guests. Local businessman H. M. Booker then purchased the establishment and made substantial renovations after a fire damaged the three upper floors in December 1896. Booker sold the Sherwood Inn to the federal government during World War I for use as an officers' mess and quarters.

After World War I ended, the Sherwood Inn reverted to a hostelry for civilian guests, though it continued to provide meals for officers. Here is the front desk in March 1924. In 1932, Randolph Hall (Building 87) opened as bachelor officers' quarters, so the Sherwood Inn was condemned and demolished. The site is now known as Sherwood Park.

In 1935, a herd of sheep and five shepherds were borrowed from nearby Fort Eustis to keep the grass cut at Fort Monroe. The post adjutant later concluded that members of the fort's two Civilian Conservation Corps camps could do the job much cheaper and terminated the program on October 10.

A snow-shoveling crew stands on the edge of the parade ground, ready to clear the walks to the barracks in this photograph, probably taken in the early 1920s. The artillery piece behind them is a French 75-millimeter gun from World War I. This weapon is now on display outside the Bay Breeze Community Center, formerly known as the Fort Monroe Officers' Club.

This wintertime view from the 1930s depicts the rebuilt main sallyport bridge, with the Hotel Chamberlin at upper left and the Fort Monroe YMCA on the right. Two trucks are about to pass each other on the bridge. The heavy snowfall seen here has become a rarity in recent years.

Military bands have always been important at Fort Monroe, and many of them were photographed for posterity. Here is the 12th Coast Artillery Regiment Band seated in front of its barracks on July 30, 1928. In 1932, this unit was replaced by the 2nd Coast Artillery Regiment Band, which was given the first opportunity to perform in the gazebo that has been used by all successive bands here.

Five

TRAINING FOR WAR
1941–1945

The onset of World War II revitalized Fort Monroe's role as a coast defense training facility. Extensive practice firing of antiaircraft guns became the norm for many Coast Artillery Corps batteries. Two Fort Monroe Coast Artillery (Antiaircraft) regiments, the 70th and 74th, eventually made their way overseas and saw action at Guadalcanal, North Africa, and Sardinia. During this time, the defense of Chesapeake Bay was expanded to include long-range guns at Fort Wool, Fort Story, and Fort John Custis. In addition, controlled mines and submarine nets were employed to ward off potential German U-boat attacks. On March 1, 1942, an anti-motor torpedo net was installed from Fort Monroe on the north to Willoughby Spit on the south, with a gate in the main channel.

The end of 1942 marked the beginning of a major scrap drive that wiped out most of Fort Monroe's historic armament. More than 2 million pounds of scrap metal were produced from Fort Monroe alone and used for the war effort. Along with old smoothbore cannons, 12-inch mortars and 12-inch rifles were added to the pile. By the end of the war, only four muzzle-loading Rodman guns and two 32-pounders remained of the original heavy armament at Fort Monroe. In 1943, more than 5,100 troops were stationed at Fort Monroe, and once again the post was bustling with activity that had a major impact on its operation. Throughout the war, the Coast Artillery School continued to operate. New courses were added, and the program was expanded with the establishment of the U.S. Officer Candidate School. A radar school for enlisted men was also established here during the war.

By the end of World War II, the modernization of the harbor defenses at Hampton Roads was nearly complete, establishing the Harbor Defense of Chesapeake Bay as the most powerful on the East Coast. However, the advancement of airplanes, submarines, and sophisticated weaponry presented a new set of challenges for harbor defenses and eventually led to the demise of the fort's two most important missions.

Brig. Gen. Rollin L. Tilton arrived at Fort Monroe in November 1940 to command the U.S. Harbor Defenses of Chesapeake Bay. On New Year's Day in 1941, he also assumed leadership of the 3rd Coast Artillery District, which became the Chesapeake Bay Sector after the Japanese attack on Pearl Harbor. Tilton held this command until it was inactivated in February 1944. He then resumed command of the Harbor Defenses of Chesapeake Bay until June 1946.

Antiaircraft artillery troops and vehicles parade down Ingalls Road at Fort Monroe on a cold day in late 1942. This image confirms the growing importance of antiaircraft artillery at the fort and other Coast Artillery Corps installations. Indeed, as World War II continued, many Coast Artillery Corps regiments were broken up and designated as antiaircraft artillery battalions.

Members of an unidentified unit line up for inspection in front of their barracks. Note the Chesapeake Bay Sector shoulder patch worn by each man. In spite of its name, this sector did not completely cover the bay, but it did include the Atlantic coast almost as far south as Wilmington, North Carolina.

A 12-inch disappearing gun fires its projectile at either Battery DeRussy or Parrott on December 6, 1942. This type of weapon was already considered outmoded for defense purposes but was still used in training exercises. Within a few years, all of these heavy artillery guns and even some of their concrete batteries would be gone.

One of the fort's best-known mascots was Sergeant Patches. The clever canine was taught to pull the lanyard that fired a 12-inch disappearing gun at Battery DeRussy. The water on the floor came from scrubbing the breech of the gun, not from the dog's indiscretion. This image is from about 1942.

With increased emphasis on antiaircraft artillery and railway guns, the Endicott batteries at Fort Monroe were considered obsolete. In March 1943, the two 12-inch disappearing guns at Battery Parrott were removed and cut up for scrap metal. Two months later, the fort's 12-inch mortars were also consigned to the scrap drive.

Crewmembers man a 3-inch antiaircraft gun along the Hampton Roads harbor, probably in 1942. By this time, the emphasis in U.S. Coast Artillery had shifted entirely from fixed heavy artillery to antiaircraft defense. Significantly, the Coast Artillery Corps was eventually succeeded by the Air Defense Artillery.

Two 155-millimeter guns and their crews perform a training exercise along the Fort Monroe waterfront in 1942. These guns were widely used by U.S. soldiers in the Field Artillery Corps as well as the Coast Artillery Corps. They could be moved and installed very quickly, though their effectiveness in places like Fort Monroe could be questioned.

Troops assigned to the Coast Artillery School Detachment are shown in formation on one of Fort Monroe's main streets. Officers and enlisted men who attended this school were assigned to this unit during the length of the school term. Most students came from Coast Artillery Corps units, though men from other branches of the service and even some foreigners occasionally enrolled.

A U.S. military police squad performs riot-duty maneuvers on the parade ground. This news photograph is dated May 4, 1942, but was probably taken several months earlier, judging by the bare tree limbs. World War II was the beginning of a military police (MP) presence at Fort Monroe, and an MP unit is still stationed at the post.

Members of the 2nd Coast Artillery Regiment Band exchange their musical instruments for gas masks in this 1942 training exercise. The men are standing along the shore of the Chesapeake Bay near Fort Monroe's firing range, a place known as Wilson Park. Note the observation platforms and other structures in the background.

As part of their Officer Candidate School (OCS) training, these students are shown how to adjust gunnery fire. The OCS program at Fort Monroe was initiated in July 1941 because West Point and Reserve Officer Training Corps (ROTC) could not furnish enough army officers for an expanded military force.

Troops clustered on the edge of the parade ground in 1942 to receive instructions on how to assault a fortified position. In September of that year, Fort Monroe staged a mock invasion of the post in which planes dropped sacks of flour and commandos scaled the moat walls. The "invaders" were stopped near the sector headquarters. Another invasion in November produced much better results.

Capt. Blaine Young instructs a group of gunnery officers in one of Fort Monroe's concrete gun batteries. This is one of the few surviving images taken inside one of these batteries. Long before World War II ended, most of these structures were abandoned.

In response to the war in Europe and possible mobilization of the Virginia National Guard, Virginia governor James Price authorized the creation of a new state military organization, the Virginia Protective Force, in January 1941. The Hampton unit is shown training on the Fort Monroe parade ground, with Building 5 in the background. In 1944, this force became the Virginia State Guard, and it was deactivated in 1947. (Courtesy of Hampton History Museum.)

Firemen pose with their truck inside the moat area of Fort Monroe in June 1941. On an installation loaded with munitions, gunpowder, and many wooden buildings, a well-trained fire department was essential. Sabotage was always a possibility, though there is no evidence that it ever took place here.

The Fort Monroe Fire Department, manned by members of the 74th Coast Artillery Regiment, performs a drill near historic Quarters No. 1 in June 1941. At that time, units assigned to the fort were responsible for firefighting duties. In later years, the fort established a civilian-operated fire department.

Enlisted men from the 74th Coast Artillery Regiment hold a fire drill in June 1941 at one of Fort Monroe's concrete gun batteries, while gun crewmen look on. This regiment was tasked with operating the post fire department. This image was donated to the Casemate Museum by Richard Taylor, who served with the unit at that time.

This postcard view of Fort Monroe in 1942 or 1943 includes the YMCA at left, the St. Mary Star-of-the-Sea Church and the main sallyport bridge at center, and two sets of quarters in the upper right. As in World War I, the fort was extremely crowded at this time, even if this image does not suggest such problems.

The soda fountain at the U.S. Army YMCA was always popular during the war. One lone civilian in the crowd looks rather out of place here. In its early years, this facility presented films, sponsored music programs, and conducted classes in various subjects, but by World War II, it had largely become a place for snacking, dancing, and exercising.

World War II brought professional entertainment to Fort Monroe. In this candid shot, bandleader Ina Ray Hutton prepares for a free concert at the post theater on April 13, 1943. A portion of the show was broadcasted on a popular Blue Network program, *The Victory Parade of Spotlight Bands*. During the concert, Pvt. Dennis Carmichael, who had sung with the late Bunny Berigan's band, was invited to perform several numbers.

Here is a typical dinner party at the Officers' (Casemate) Club during World War II. This is from a collection of photographs donated to the Casemate Museum by Rollin Tilton, who was the fort's commanding general at that time. Unfortunately, the officers and (presumably) their wives are not identified, but they all seem to be having a good time. The pack of Lucky Strikes on the table reminds us that this was an era of heavy smokers.

Servicemen and their ladies dance cheek to cheek at the Fort Monroe YMCA during World War II. This was the place to go for social activities then. The young woman in the foreground does not seem too thrilled to have her picture taken. Note the Chesapeake Bay Sector shoulder patch on her partner's uniform.

This rare interior shot of the Officers' Beach Club was taken during a farewell luncheon sponsored by the Fort Monroe Red Cross Chapter for Lena Clark, the wife of Brig. Gen. Frank S. Clark, in August 1942. Lena Clark is seated at the far end of the table on the right. Next to her and facing the camera, is Kathleen Tilton, whose husband commanded the Chesapeake Bay Sector during World War II.

The original Fort Monroe Officers' Beach Club was destroyed by a fire of undetermined origin on July 15, 1944. Enemy sabotage was not suspected. A large tent was erected so that patrons could continue to use the site and the undamaged outdoor pool. A new and much larger club building was completed by May 1945.

The 2nd Coast Artillery Regiment Band performs at a flag-raising ceremony at the flagstaff bastion, where Fort Monroe's garrison flag has always flown. This unit was the official fort band between April 1932 and May 1944. It then became the 69th Army Ground Forces Band and remained here for two more years.

On November 24, 1942, an honor guard is formed to welcome Lord Halifax, the British ambassador to the United States and former foreign secretary in Prime Minister Neville Chamberlin's cabinet. In the background are the news depot on the steamship wharf, a gazebo that is still used for band concerts, and the Hotel Chamberlin, which became a facility for transient naval officers (including Lt. Douglas Fairbanks Jr.) during the war.

Red Cross volunteers hold a planning session in Building 20 or 21 in 1942. This program began to play an important role at Fort Monroe at that time and remains so even today. Lena Clark, wife of the Coast Artillery School commandant, organized the local chapter and devoted much time and energy to it.

Two Red Cross nurses brief an unidentified woman wearing a Coast Artillery Corps pin (far left) and Kathleen Tilton (second from right), the wife of Brig. Gen. Rollin Tilton, the Chesapeake Bay Sector commander during World War II. Kathleen Tilton was probably much more popular than her husband, whose no-nonsense attitude was not always appreciated.

Four enlisted men are shown behind a pile of sandbags along Fort Monroe's beach road. These GIs are not identified but are quite typical of the countless numbers of soldiers who passed through the fort during World War II. Most of them left even less evidence of their presence than this snapshot.

A soldier carries his standard-issue Springfield rifle with fixed bayonet. Behind him is a row of barracks for Officer Candidate School (OCS) students. The attack on Pearl Harbor led to much tighter security at all American military bases, and Fort Monroe was no exception.

A new student at Officer Candidate School (OCS) meets some old hands in autumn 1942. Hundreds of students successfully completed this program at Fort Monroe and then served in the war effort. This image comes from a booklet titled, "Fort Monroe and the Coast Artillery School."

Two soldiers pose on the balcony of their temporary barracks building while another man starts to climb down the ladder and a fourth soldier sits nonchalantly on a fence rail. Many of these buildings were still in use as offices through the 1990s, but all of them have now been removed.

This display of weapons and observation instruments was set up for U.S. Army Day at Fort Monroe, probably on June 14, 1942. An OCS candidate sent this postcard to a friend in Wilmington, Delaware, telling him that, "I was gigged this week-end for a dirty rifle, so I am not allowed on pass. Ha, Ha. This is a picture of the kind of gun I was working with all week." The card is postmarked on March 1, 1943.

Here are four civilian crewmembers of Fort Monroe's railroad system in 1944. They are standing in front of locomotive 4021. This system was created to service the fort's gun batteries with its short lines and rather modest rail stock, but it eventually developed into much more of a state-of-the-art operation.

Five soldiers at Fort Monroe wait patiently for the steamer that will transport them across the Chesapeake Bay to Cape Charles on Virginia's Eastern Shore and points north. During World War II, this was a major means of transportation, in addition to the Chesapeake and Ohio rail line at nearby Phoebus.

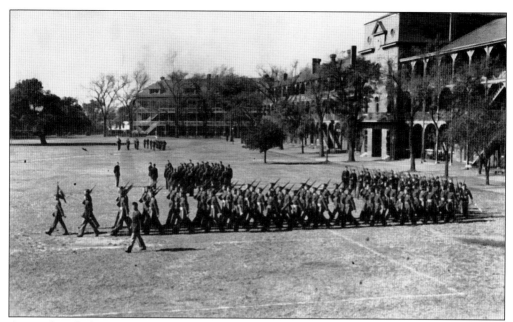

An unidentified Coast Artillery Corps unit drills on the parade ground. In the background is Building 10 and at right is Building 5; both served as unit barracks at the time. Building 5, the largest structure inside the moat area, was completed in 1879 but underwent so many alterations by World War II that it became almost unrecognizable.

Batteries of the 2nd Coast Artillery Regiment are shown in formation on the parade ground in this c. 1942 photograph. This regiment was stationed at Fort Monroe from 1932 to 1944 and then was downsized into a battalion for another year before deactivation. The imposing structure in the background is Building 5, which served as a unit barracks from 1879 until 1955, when it was converted into an office building.

Six

AN ERA ENDS AND NEW MISSIONS BEGIN
1946–1972

By 1945, the Coast Artillery Corps had largely been transformed into an antiaircraft defense branch. Fort Monroe's commander, Brig. Gen. Rollin Tilton, acknowledged that the Coast Artillery School facilities were inadequate for this mission. In June 1946, after graduation exercises, the Coast Artillery School relocated to Fort Winfield Scott, California. The following year U.S. Army Ground Forces decreed that all harbor defense operations be shut down, and Fort Monroe's armament was quickly reduced. On January 1, 1950, the Coast Artillery Corps was officially inactivated. The 4th battalion of the 51st Artillery (antiaircraft) was the last artillery unit to serve at Fort Monroe, ending its service on July 26, 1960. The end of the Coast Artillery Corps at Fort Monroe coincided with other breaks in tradition. In 1959, due to maintenance problems and overcrowding, the historic Officers' (Casemate) Club was closed and moved to the Officers' Beach Club. Since 1871, this famous facility had been located inside the flagstaff bastion. The Hotel Chamberlin, which was operated by the U.S. Navy during World War II, was sold in 1947 to L. U. Noland, the operator of a chain of hotels in Richmond. In addition, Fort Monroe's main dock, popularly known as the Baltimore Wharf, was demolished in 1961 after serving military personnel and civilians since 1894. Nevertheless, interest was generated to begin preserving, interpreting, and exhibiting the rich history of Fort Monroe. Through the efforts of Dr. Chester Bradley and post commander Col. Paul R. Goode, the Jefferson Davis Casemate Museum was opened on June 1, 1951. At first it displayed only the cell where the Confederate leader had been imprisoned after the Civil War, but within three years, this facility expanded and became the Casemate Museum. In an important step to preserve its rich history, Fort Monroe was declared a National Historic Landmark on December 19, 1960. During this time, new commands were established at Fort Monroe, including the Army Ground Forces (1946–1948), the Army Field Forces (1948–1955), and the Continental Army Command (CONARC) (1955–1973). All these commands were responsible for operation, training, and administrative functions for the entire U.S. Army.

Here is a view of Fort Monroe's main gate during the period when it served as the headquarters for the Continental Army Command (1955–1973). The entrance has become more elaborate, but the guard shack is still in use. Due to heightened security concern, the fort now has two main gates, one for "official" traffic and one for vendors and visitors.

The 50th Army Band was stationed here from November 1946 to June 1972. The unit is shown in dress blues for a ceremony on the parade ground in 1956. For some reason, bands at Fort Monroe are much better documented than many other units that have been stationed here over the years.

By 1951, the moat surrounding the original fort had accumulated layers of silt and muck, so a decision was made to drain the moat and dredge it. The stench resulting from this project caused so many complaints that a similar plan was never carried out again. Here a small steam shovel is operating at the end of a makeshift roadway. In the background is the North Gate Bridge.

This image provides the viewer with an appreciation for the extent of the moat-dredging project in 1951. Patch Road runs from right to center, and the North Gate Bridge can be seen near the upper left corner. In the mid-1970s, U.S. Army divers from Fort Eustis removed cannonballs, bottles, and other old items from the moat.

The Old Bay Line continued to operate steamships between Old Point Comfort and points north, but its years were numbered. Members of the graduating class of St. Vincent's Catholic High School in Newport News pose on the wharf before embarking on their senior class trip in the spring of 1956.

This view of the Baltimore Wharf at Old Point Comfort probably dates from 1959, when steamship service ended. A sign over the open door states "PARK AT OWN RISK," which appears to be good advice. The completion of the Hampton Roads Bridge Tunnel between Hampton and Norfolk in 1957 sealed the fate of steamer traffic in this area.

After the Old Bay Line discontinued operations at Fort Monroe, the wharf deteriorated to the extent that a decision was made to demolish it before any serious accidents might happen. Only the outlines of this once bustling transportation facility can be seen in this February 1961 image.

After World War II, the U. S. Navy relinquished control of the Hotel Chamberlin. The army attempted to acquire the property but was rebuffed by the U.S. War Department. The hotel returned to its original status as a resort facility. The outdoor swimming pool was a popular place when this picture was taken, which was probably in the mid-1950s.

In February 1946, two 3-inch antiaircraft guns were dismantled and taken from Battery Irwin, leaving holes in each emplacement. This battery fared better than its companions because, on May 31, 1946, two 3-inch barbette guns with armor shields were transported from Battery Lee at nearby Fort Wool and installed at Irwin as salute guns. They are still in place today.

Battery DeRussy, once a major component in Fort Monroe's coast defense arsenal, was just another abandoned, boarded-up building on March 24, 1959, when this image was taken. The battery was opened for weekend tours during the late 1970s, but internal deterioration has now made it off-limits.

In December 1949, Dr. Chester Bradley, a local pediatrician and history buff, gave a speech suggesting that Fort Monroe restore the cell where Jefferson Davis had been incarcerated and open it to the public. On June 1, 1951, this idea became a reality with a dedication ceremony on the parade ground. The keynote speaker, shown here, was the Confederate president's grandson, Jefferson Hayes-Davis, who traveled from Colorado Springs, Colorado, for this occasion.

The opening of the Jefferson Davis Casemate Museum (as the facility was known at that time) was timed to coincide with the 61st reunion of Confederate veterans in Norfolk. Several of them, including William J. Bush of Fitzgerald, Georgia, made the trip to Old Point Comfort by steamer for the ceremony.

Jefferson Hayes-Davis sits on a cot in the same cell where his grandfather was imprisoned from May to October 1865. He is flanked by reenactors portraying the two Union soldiers who guarded Jefferson Davis each day and night. Hayes-Davis also donated several Davis artifacts that are now on permanent display at the Casemate Museum.

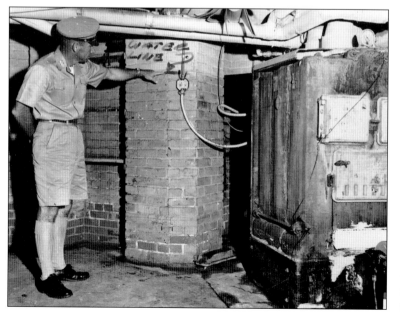

Severe storms and floods continued to create problems at Fort Monroe. This officer points to the extent of water in his basement in 1956 due to inadequate drainage systems. People are often surprised to learn that many buildings on the post have basements, though most consist of furnace rooms such as this one.

In December 1960, the federal government declared Fort Monroe to be a National Historic Landmark. On May 9, 1961, the official certificate declaring this action was presented at a ceremony inside the Casemate Museum. Participants from left to right are Harold S. Shiffen (museum committee member), Miriam Bradley, Malvin C. Weaver (museum committee member), Dr. Chester Bradley (museum curator), Dr. Stanley Abbott (National Park Service), Col. Paul R. Jeffrey (post commander), Irving L. Fuller (museum committee member), and Bea Kopp (*Newport News Daily Press* photographer). This action of course preceded passage of the National Historic Landmark Act of 1966, which is now interpreted to include Fort Monroe in its provisions. This has significant implications for enactment of the Base Realignment and Closing (BRAC) measures regarding future use of the fort.

The extent of flooding in 1962 can be seen in this view of the parking area between Building 11 and the post commissary. Despite the seawall, sandbagging operations, and other preventive measures, floods remain a serious challenge for Fort Monroe, which is a floodplain site completely surrounded by salt water.

In late September 1972, a record-breaking flash flood hit the Virginia peninsula. This aerial view of Fort Monroe shows the consequences. Note the parade ground in the center, which has become a lake with a small island. Beyond the fort is the Hampton Roads Bridge-Tunnel connecting Hampton and Norfolk.

The aftermath of a severe flood at Fort Monroe can be seen in this image, taken on September 21, 1972. The parade ground has become a muddy lake, with water coming all the way up to the former barracks buildings in the background. Between the live oak trees, a woman and her husband slog through the water. Note that the man is carrying the family dog.

Here is a closer view of the parade ground after a severe storm hit Fort Monroe in September 1972. The man at lower center appears to be examining his car for damage. Near the right margin, a boy stands on the only piece of dry land in sight while his friend wades into the water. This area of the fort is still prone to flooding after heavy rains.

In this *c.* 1970 photograph, this young man seems anxious to open his holiday gift (something called a Funny Pumper) at this Christmas party for Fort Monroe dependents. More recent traditions each December include the lighting of the post Christmas tree, the arrival of Santa Claus on a fire truck, and the holiday band concert.

This group photograph from May 13, 1969, shows five members of Fort Monroe Girl Scout Troop 4 who were recently promoted to First Class Scouts, with their advisor, Maj. Joann Strong (far left). From left to right, the girls are Kathie Bartley, Patty Krist, unidentified, Kathy Fitzgerald, Brenda Ashby, and Lynn Reudelhuber.

Carol Cavanaugh, the daughter of Q.M. Sgt. John Cavanaugh, stands outside Building T-252 on Buckner Street in 1950. This temporary structure served as enlisted housing at the time but has since been demolished. Carol's mother, Mary Cavanaugh, walks across the lawn. Carol was born in the Fort Monroe hospital and returned to the post years later to work as a secretary.

Female soldiers of the Fort Monroe WAC Company, Continental Army Command, march in formation around 1970. This was perhaps a ceremonial occasion, judging by the spectators lined up along the curb. The establishment of an all-volunteer military force in 1974 brought an end to the U.S. Women's Army Corps, which had been a presence at Fort Monroe since 1946.

Fort Monroe's most notable social event occurred on June 10, 1947, when Barbara Thompson and Capt. John Eisenhower were married in the post chapel. Barbara's father, a colonel, was stationed here at the time, while Captain Eisenhower was the son of Gen. Dwight D. and Mamie Eisenhower. Here the couple receives a military police salute following the ceremony.

Easter sunrise service at Continental Park has been an annual event at Fort Monroe since the early 1950s. This U. S. Army photograph is undated but probably comes from the late 1950s. In recent years, attendance has declined, probably due to security concerns and an increase in the number of sunrise services elsewhere.

Seven

THE ROAD AHEAD
1973–PRESENT

In an effort to streamline command positions, the U.S. Army reorganized the functions of the Continental Army Command (CONARC). The plan called for creating two new organizations, the Army Forces Command (FORSCOM) and the Training and Doctrine Command (TRADOC). TRADOC was established at Fort Monroe on July 1, 1973, with Gen. William E. DePuy as its first commanding general. TRADOC brought together the activities by which troops and leaders are trained, doctrine formulated, units built, and weapons requirements refined. An important Field Manual 100-5 (Operations) was created on July 1, 1976, which introduced the doctrine of active defense. In March 1979, after a comprehensive study of base realignments and closures (BRAC), the army proposed moving TRADOC to Fort Eustis. After three years of study, the army argued that Fort Monroe would be more expensive to close than to keep it open. Secretary of the U.S. Army John O. Marsh announced on September 23, 1981, that the post would be retained because of "the complicated real property situation and the unquestioned need to preserve, for the public, the significant heritage that Fort Monroe represents." The decision to keep Fort Monroe an active army installation made it possible to undertake necessary repairs to roads, sewers, and buildings, which were brought up to modern standards. A variety of new commands found a home at Fort Monroe, including the U.S. Army Cadet Command, the U.S. Army Accessions Command, the Naval Surface Warfare Center, the Joint Task Force–Civil Support, and the Installation Management Command (Northeast Region). On September 18, 2003, Fort Monroe suffered through another disaster with Hurricane Isabel slamming down on the Hampton Roads area and mid-Atlantic states. Major flooding occurred on Fort Monroe, leaving behind nearly $100 million worth of damage to roads, buildings, and key infrastructures. Once again, Fort Monroe was able to rebuild and move forward. On September 15, 2005, U.S. president George W. Bush approved the BRAC commission's recommendations to close Fort Monroe. Congress had 45 days to disapprove the list or it would automatically become binding. Congress did not disapprove the list within the time allotted, and Fort Monroe was scheduled to close in September 2011. Although the fort will no longer be an active military installation, the work conducted by the units will continue at other military installations.

On July 1, 1973, the headquarters for Training and Doctrine Command (TRADOC) was established at Fort Monroe with Gen. William E. DePuy pictured here (left) as the commander. This ceremony at Continental Park made it official. Known as the founder of TRADOC, he spearheaded what was perhaps the most dramatic single advance in tactics, doctrine, equipment, modernization, and training ever undertaken by a peacetime army. Before leading TRADOC, General DePuy served in World War II with the 90th Infantry Division and commanded the 1st Infantry Division during the Vietnam War from 1966 to 1967. Retiring in 1977, he continued to influence the direction of the army and TRADOC as a military affairs writer, lecturer, and advisor. Recognized as one of the great U.S. Army leaders of his time, he died at Arlington, Virginia, on September 9, 1992. His legacy was the trained and ready army that went to Panama in Operation Just Cause in 1989 and the Persian Gulf in 1990–1991.

On August 24, 1973, General DePuy congratulates a finalist in the U.S. Army Drill Sergeant of the Year competition at Fort Monroe, while the sergeant's wife looks on. TRADOC's mission oversees the training of army drill sergeants all across the United States and is responsible for conducting basic training for incoming soldiers, a mission that continues today.

To celebrate the nation's bicentennial in 1976, Fort Monroe created a reenactment group known as Gaskins' Battalion. These men represent the artillery element of that unit. They are shown on the parade ground next to a period 12-pounder cannon on a reproduction carriage.

The Casemate Museum sponsored annual Civil War reenactment camps at Fort Monroe between 1987 and 1990. In this event from May 1989, a fife-and-drum unit plays period music on the parade ground. The men are depicting Union army troops, since Fort Monroe remained a Union stronghold throughout the war.

The first Civil War reenactment event at Fort Monroe was scheduled to coincide with the 125th anniversary of the famous battle in March 1862 between the USS *Monitor* and the CSS *Virginia* (formerly *Merrimack*). Here an artillery unit prepares to fire a 12-pounder howitzer at Continental Park.

TRADOC Organization Day in late June includes a Historical Walking Tour of notable Fort Monroe sites sponsored by the Casemate Museum. As part of the 1998 tour, museum docent Judith Connelly discussed the history of the post chapel. Other locations included the flagstaff bastion, the stockade, Quarters No. 1, and the lighthouse.

In May 1995, Congressman Newt Gingrich of Georgia visited Fort Monroe. The recently elected speaker of the House of Representatives was the highest-ranking federal official to make an official visit to the fort since U.S. president Franklin Roosevelt in 1940. He is shown here with Gen. William Hartzog, commanding general of the Training and Doctrine Command (TRADOC), which was headquartered at this post.

The tour program at the Casemate Museum depends almost exclusively on volunteers known as docents. Each year the museum revises its tour guide manual and sponsors a seminar for prospective docents with training provided by graduates of the program. Here Rexa Lee Pickett discusses a 12-pounder Confederate cannon with newcomers Pat Bergeron, Janet Aurentz, and Sally Gregerson, while veteran docent Vicki Andrews looks on. For many years, the museum relied on officers' wives, such as this group in April 1984, to maintain the tour program, but changing economic and social factors have virtually dried up that particular talent pool. Today military and civilian retirees make up the largest percentage of the museum docent force, and that situation is unlikely to change in the near future.

For National Library Week in April 1995, Bobbi Hartzog, the wife of TRADOC commanding general William Hartzog, interacts with a group of young patrons at the Fort Monroe Library. This facility carries on the tradition of the U.S. Artillery School Library and its many successors at the fort.

Officer McGruff, the crime-fighting dog, has been a familiar sight at Kids' Day and other Fort Monroe activities for many years. Here he interacts with a group of young people along the waterfront in August 1993. Kids Day allows family members and the community to experience various programs put on by the U.S. Army.

One of the highlights of each Civil War reenactment camp at Fort Monroe was the Saturday retreat ceremony. Soldiers lined the ramp leading to the flagstaff bastion as two officers hauled down the garrison flag and carefully folded it. The ceremony shown here took place on May 13, 1989.

Prior to "church call" on Sunday morning, Civil War reenactment units at Fort Monroe were usually inspected by the post commander. Here Col. Eugene Scott examines an infantryman's rifle-musket as Lt. Robert Frey looks on. This event occurred on the parade ground on May 14, 1989.

Since 1994, the most important children's event at Fort Monroe has been Kids Day, which is always held on the parade ground in August. The 2000 edition featured traditional sack races for different age groups, as well as more contemporary activities, and a variety of food. (Courtesy of Army Community Services.)

OpSail was a major event along the East Coast of the United States in 2000. On June 16, the long line of sailing ships passed Old Point Comfort on its way to Norfolk. Fort Monroe residents, workers, and visitors had an excellent view of this spectacle, especially from the fishing pier. (Courtesy of Claire Samuelson.)

The highlight of each TRADOC Organization Day schedule is a championship softball game. In this contest, Maj. Dominick Nutter of the garrison team bats against the DCSPIL (Deputy Chief of Staff for Personnel, Infrastructure and Logistics) team on June 29, 2007. The result was not exactly a cliffhanger, with the garrison team winning 11–0. (Courtesy of Fort Monroe Public Affairs Office.)

Children's activities at Fort Monroe include many diverse events. In this flag football game sponsored by Youth Sports, Tyler DiCola of the Fort Monroe Ravens heads to the goal post with several Fort Eustis Patriots in hot pursuit. This game for boys aged five to seven was played at Walker Airfield on July 24, 2007. (Courtesy of Fort Monroe Public Affairs Office.)

Fort Monroe has not suffered greatly from fire damage in recent decades, but this conflagration was a rare exception. On October 1, 1981, fire broke out in the yacht club building and quickly spread along the length of the marina, destroying many boats and parked vehicles. Black smoke from this disaster drifted all over the post for hours. The entire marina has since been rebuilt and expanded.

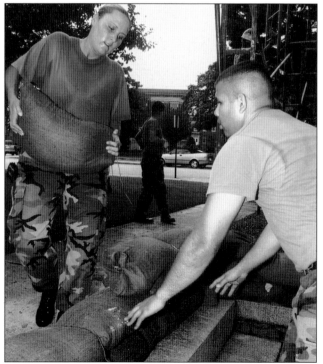

Two soldiers carry out the laborious task of stacking sandbags around a basement entrance to Building 83, the former post office. This process was repeated all around Fort Monroe as Hurricane Isabel made its way slowly up the southeastern coast. The fort's proximity to Hampton Roads, the Chesapeake Bay, and Mill Creek made this situation especially alarming. (Courtesy of Fort Monroe Public Affairs Office.)

Hurricane Isabel struck Fort Monroe on the night of September 18, 2003, during high tide and after a period of heavy rainfall that had already saturated the ground. This deadly combination caused more damage to the fort than any storm since 1933. Here an enlisted man from the Chapel Center attempts to remove debris from the front of the post chapel. (Courtesy of Fort Monroe Public Affairs Office.)

A Fort Monroe soldier wades through floodwater along Ingalls Road while a comrade looks at him, perhaps thinking better of the idea. This photograph was probably shot soon after Hurricane Isabel did considerable damage to the post on September 18, 2003. Many quarters, offices, and vehicles were flooded, which necessitated a multi-million dollar cleanup. (Courtesy of Fort Monroe Environmental Office.)

In early October 2007, the Casemate Museum sponsored a weekend event marking the 100th anniversary of the establishment of the Coast Artillery Corps as a separate branch of the army. This was the first time since 1990 that a military reenactment group was invited to participate. The Army Ground Forces Association brought vehicles, equipment, 1930s-period uniforms, and expertise to the event, making it a great success. Here Andy Bennett explains the operation of a Swasey depression position finder to a visitor.

The TRADOC (Training and Doctrine Command) Band in full regalia poses in front of Quarters No. 1, the oldest surviving army building at Fort Monroe. This ensemble travels extensively, gives workshops for young musicians, and provides support for virtually all official ceremonies at the fort. The band is best known for its annual series of summer concerts at the gazebo in Continental Park, continuing a tradition that began in 1934. (Courtesy of the U.S. Army TRADOC Band.)

Sfc. Rodney Noe greets workers, tenants, and visitors at Fort Monroe's main gate on June 26, 1992. Security measures at the fort were relatively relaxed then but have changed significantly since the tragic events of September 11, 2001. The guard shack is still in operation for vehicles with official decals, but another guard post has been set up to screen all other traffic. (Courtesy of the Fort Monroe Public Affairs Office.)

The water in the moat, which is fed through a sluice gate from Mill Creek, calmly moves around the Second Front of Fort Monroe at sunset. The army's departure from Fort Monroe, based on the BRAC decision in 2005, leaves behind a rich legacy of service to the United States. This photograph was taken in 1995. (Courtesy of the Fort Monroe Public Affairs Office.)

ACROSS AMERICA, PEOPLE ARE DISCOVERING
SOMETHING WONDERFUL. THEIR HERITAGE.

Arcadia Publishing is the leading local history publisher in the United States. With more than 4,000 titles in print and hundreds of new titles released every year, Arcadia has extensive specialized experience chronicling the history of communities and celebrating America's hidden stories, bringing to life the people, places, and events from the past. To discover the history of other communities across the nation, please visit:

www.arcadiapublishing.com

Customized search tools allow you to find regional history books about the town where you grew up, the cities where your friends and family live, the town where your parents met, or even that retirement spot you've been dreaming about.

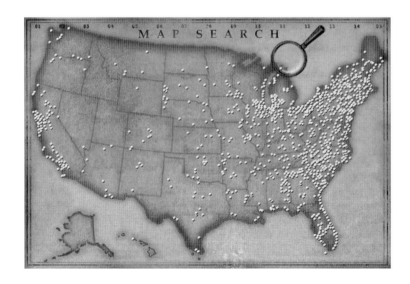